SMART WORDS
READER

Life in the Tundra

Christine A. Caputo

SCHOLASTIC INC.

What are SMART WORDS?

Smart Words are frequently used words that are critical to understanding concepts taught in the classroom. The more Smart Words a child knows, the more easily he or she will grasp important curriculum concepts. Smart Words Readers introduce these key words in a fun and motivational format while developing important literacy skills. Each new word is highlighted, defined in context, and reviewed. Engaging activities at the end of each chapter allow readers to practice the words they have learned.

Title page photo: A reindeer on the tundra

No part of this publication may be reproduced, stored in a retrieval system, or transmitted in any form or by any means, electronic, mechanical, photocopying, recording, or otherwise, without written permission of the publisher. For information regarding permission, write to Scholastic Inc., Attention: Permissions Department, 557 Broadway, New York, NY 10012.

ISBN 978-0-545-59641-1

Packaged by Q2A Bill Smith

Series Editor: Nikki Bruno Clapper

Copyright © 2013 by Scholastic Inc.

Picture Credit: t= top, b= bottom, l= left, r= right, c= center

Cover Page: Mogens Trolle/Shutterstock

Title Page: Erectus/Dreamstime.com

Contents Page: Sergey Uryadnikov/Shutterstock

4–5: Hanjon02/Dreamstime; 5: Baszer/Dreamstime; 6: Sergey Shulga/Shutterstock; 7: Tomtsya/Shutterstock; 9: Jiri Kasal/Dreamstime; 11: John E Marriott/All Canada Photos/Glow Images; 12–13: Nick Jans/AlaskaStock RM/Glow Images; 15: Noaa; 16: Nathan Jaskowiak/Shutterstock; 17: kavram/Shutterstock; 18: Calamityjohn/ Dreamstime; 19: Fabio Lotti/Shutterstock; 20l: Cabinpress/Dreamstime; 20r: WayneDuguay/Shutterstock; 21t: John Sylvester/All Canada Photos/Glow Images; 21b: Wayne Lynch/All Canada Photos/Glow Images; 22: Twildlife/Dreamstime; 23tr: FloridaStock/Shutterstock; 23tl: Power and Syred/Science Photo Library; 24: Vidux/Shutterstock; 25: Neil Harrison/Dreamstime; 26: Shirley Palmer/123RF; 27: Outdoosman/Shutterstock; 28: FloridaStock/Shutterstock; 29: Sergey Krasnoshchokov/Shutterstock; 30–31: Iakov Kalinin/Dreamstime

Q2A Bill Smith Art Bank: 8; 11; 12; 14

12 11 10 9 8 7 6 5 4 3   13 14 15 16 17 18/0

Printed in the U.S.A.   40

First printing, September 2013

Table of Contents

Chapter 1

Deep Freeze!

Bundle up! You're about to visit a frozen land. You'll brave strong winds. You'll slide across thick ice. You might even see a polar bear. Welcome to the **tundra**!

The tundra is one of Earth's main **biomes**. A biome is a community of plants and animals that share a certain environment. Have you heard of the desert, the grassland, and the rain forest? These are biomes, too.

In the tundra, the cold hits you right away. This is the coldest biome on Earth.

Am I in the Tundra?

If you answer yes to all of these questions, you're probably in the tundra!

- Is the air very cold?
- Is there little rain or snow?
- Is the wind really strong?
- Are there few or no trees?
- Are plants low to the ground?

This is the tundra of Lapland, a region of northern Europe. Notice that there are no trees.

4

If you stick around, you'll see very little rain or snow. The tundra gets less than 10 inches (25 centimeters) of precipitation all year.

And if you're looking for shelter, you won't find many trees. It's just too cold for trees to grow. Instead, tundra plants grow close to the ground, in clumps or mats. The tundra's many **cushion plants** look like little pillows.

Moss is a cushion plant that blankets the tundra. Low plants that grow close together stay protected from wind and cold.

SMART WORDS

tundra a cold region with almost no trees and under 10 inches (25 centimeters) of precipitation each year

biome a community of plants and animals that share a certain environment

cushion plant a low-growing plant that forms clumps or mats

Lopsided Seasons

The tundra has two seasons — summer and winter. One is cold, and the other is colder.

In some tundra areas, the average winter temperature is -30 degrees Fahrenheit (-34 degrees Celsius). That's 30°F colder than your freezer at home! In these areas, the summer isn't very warm, either. It's rarely above 50°F (10°C), and it lasts only a few weeks.

The tundra also has a short growing season in the summer each year. Some plants need several growing seasons to mature. It can take ten years for these plants to form flower buds!

The tundra is a colorful place only at the height of its short summer. In just a few weeks, these bursts of red will be gone.

Flowing Ice

The **climate** of the tundra is perfect for **glaciers**. A glacier is a huge area of ice. It moves slowly downhill or outward over time.

A glacier forms when winter snow does not melt in summer. Over thousands of years, the snow piles up. It packs down to form a thick layer of ice.

If the world's glaciers melted, Earth would be a wet place. The glaciers hold about three-fourths of the planet's freshwater!

Iceland is a beautiful country where tundra meets glacier. About 11 percent of Iceland is covered by glacial ice. Shown here is Vatnajökull, the largest glacier in Europe.

SMART WORDS

climate the overall weather in a place over a long period of time

glacier a huge, slow-moving mass of ice

Arctic and Alpine

Where in the world do you think you can find tundra? It forms only in places that are very cold and very dry.

If you're thinking far north, you're on the right track. Much of Earth's tundra surrounds the North Pole. This type of tundra is known as **arctic** tundra. Think of places like Alaska, Canada, Greenland, and Russia.

Arctic tundra can be found in the extreme northern parts of the planet. Alpine tundra is found in mountainous regions throughout the world.

Tundra Around the World

Key

■	Artic tundra
■	Alpine tundra

The other type of tundra is called **alpine** tundra. The word *alpine* describes anything related to high mountains. If you want to find alpine tundra, you have to put on your hiking boots and climb. Think of places like the Rocky Mountains, the Himalayas of Tibet, the mountains around Africa's Great Rift Valley, and the Alps of Europe.

SMART WORDS

arctic relating to regions near the North Pole

alpine relating to high mountains

Mount Kenya is the second-highest peak on the continent of Africa. Many unusual plants live in its alpine tundra biome.

Match each description to the correct Smart Word.

> tundra biome cushion plant
>
> climate glacier arctic alpine

1. the long-term weather conditions of a place

2. a community of plants and animals that live in a certain environment

3. a cold, dry region with almost no trees

4. a type of plant that grows in clumps low to the ground

5. a description of high mountains

6. a description of something that is near the North Pole

7. a slow-moving body of ice

Answers on page 32

Talk Like a Scientist

Use your Smart Words to tell your family what the tundra is like in summer and in winter.

SMART FACTS

Did You Know?

In some parts of the arctic tundra, the sun never sets in the summer. People say these areas have a midnight sun because the sun shines even at midnight.

That's Amazing!

During the winter, the sun never rises in parts of the arctic tundra. It looks like it is nighttime or twilight all the time. This is called the polar night.

It's All About the Tilt

Midnight suns and polar nights happen because Earth is tilted. During the summer months, the North Pole tilts toward the sun. During wintertime, the North Pole points away from the sun.

Earth's tilt brings the North Pole into the sunlight in summer.

Spring

Summer

Winter

← North Pole

Sun

Fall

Chapter 2

From Pole to Peak

In winter, the arctic tundra can feel like outer space — big, cold, and far from human life. In this type of tundra, only the top layer of soil thaws in the summer. The main layer below, called **permafrost**, stays frozen all year.

Permafrost can be very thick. In parts of Siberia, an area of Russia, the permafrost is 5,000 feet (1,500 meters) thick. That's almost a mile!

Arctic Tundra Soil Layers

top layer

permafrost

In the arctic tundra, a thick layer of soil called permafrost stays frozen all year long. The ice prevents tall plants such as trees from growing.

Wicked Winds

In the arctic tundra, wind blows constantly. Much of the land is wide-open and flat. There are no trees to slow down or block the wind.

The strong winds pick up snow and carry it to other places. Big piles of snow called snow dunes can form. Sometimes, the snow moves so fast that everything looks white. This is called a **whiteout**. It can last for days at a time.

Wind can whip across the flat tundra at speeds of 30 to 60 miles per hour (48 to 96 kilometers per hour).

SMART WORDS

permafrost a layer of soil that is always frozen

whiteout a condition when high winds pick up snow and blow it around quickly so everything looks white

Warming Up

The arctic tundra biome is under threat. Scientists have noticed that Greenland's ice sheet — an enormous glacier — is melting faster than ever before. Why? One explanation is called the greenhouse effect, which is causing temperatures around the world to rise.

A greenhouse is a building made of glass. It traps the sun's heat inside so people can grow plants even when it is cold. Gases surrounding Earth act like the glass of a greenhouse. They trap heat near Earth's surface.

The Greenhouse Effect

Heat from the sun warms Earth, and some heat goes back to space

The sun's energy passes through a layer of gases

Greenhouse gases trap some heat and send it back to Earth

Human activities add a lot of extra gases to the air. For instance, we create gas when we burn coal. This causes Earth to warm up more than it would naturally. The gradual heating of the planet is called **global warming**. As the planet warms up, the ice of the arctic tundra melts.

The Greenland Ice Sheet covers 80 percent of the country — and it holds an amazing 10 percent of the world's freshwater! Huge parts of this ice sheet are melting. Many scientists say this is happening because of the greenhouse effect.

SMART WORDS

ice sheet glacial ice that covers a large area of land

greenhouse effect what happens when gases surrounding Earth trap heat near the planet's surface

global warming a trend of rising temperatures all over Earth

Tundra of the Mountains

You don't have to go to arctic regions to find tundra. You can find it in warmer areas of the world, too. But how can warmer regions get cold and dry enough to support tundra?

Climb toward the sky, and you'll have the answer. In mountain regions — even in those of warm countries — the higher you go, the colder it is. Alpine tundra is found at the tops of tall mountains. For instance, you can find alpine tundra along the peaks of the Rocky Mountains in the western United States.

Alpine tundra covers about one-third of Rocky Mountain National Park in Colorado. To reach this biome, you have to climb to about 11,000 feet (3,350 meters) above sea level.

tree line

On a high mountain, it is easy to see the tree line. Above the line, you can see only rock, ice, and snow.

Alpine tundra forms above the **tree line**. This is an imaginary line on a mountain. Above the line, it is so cold and windy that trees can't grow. From far away, the tree line is easy to spot.

Alpine tundra can be found around the globe, wherever the mountains are high enough. You can find this biome in Mexico, South America, Europe, Africa, and many other places.

SMART WORD

tree line a boundary on a mountain above which trees do not grow

Use your SMART WORDS

Read each clue. Choose the Smart Word it describes.

permafrost	whiteout	ice sheet
greenhouse effect	global warming	tree line

1. I describe an overall increase in temperatures on Earth.

2. I am a boundary on a mountain. Trees cannot grow above me.

3. I am a layer of soil that never thaws.

4. I cause extra heat to get trapped near Earth.

5. I am a glacier that covers a large area of land.

6. I am what happens when the wind blows lots of snow around.

Answers on page 32

Talk Like a Scientist

Write a short newspaper article about the two types of tundra. Use your Smart Words to express your ideas. Include a drawing.

SMART FACTS

Did You Know?

An iceberg is a large chunk that breaks off from a glacier or ice sheet.

That's Huge!

In 2010, a chunk of the Greenland Ice Sheet collapsed. The chunk was four times as big as the island of Manhattan in New York City! It was made of enough water to supply everyone in the United States for about four months.

That's Amazing!

When a piece of an ice sheet breaks off, it leaves behind an enormous cliff. The cliff left behind in Greenland was about half as tall as the Empire State Building.

Chapter 3

Wildlife of the Tundra

Some amazing animals make their home in the tundra. Over millions of years, their bodies have **adapted**, or changed in ways that help them survive. The adaptation of **camouflage** allows animals to blend in to their surroundings.

Predators are animals that hunt other animals, known as prey. Camouflage helps predators sneak up on their prey without being seen. It also helps prey hide from predators.

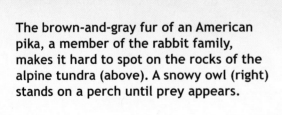

The brown-and-gray fur of an American pika, a member of the rabbit family, makes it hard to spot on the rocks of the alpine tundra (above). A snowy owl (right) stands on a perch until prey appears.

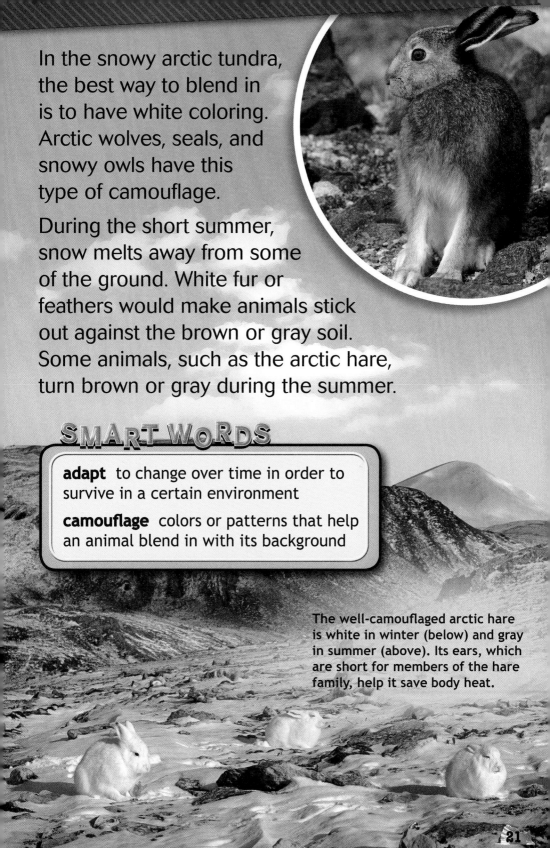

In the snowy arctic tundra, the best way to blend in is to have white coloring. Arctic wolves, seals, and snowy owls have this type of camouflage.

During the short summer, snow melts away from some of the ground. White fur or feathers would make animals stick out against the brown or gray soil. Some animals, such as the arctic hare, turn brown or gray during the summer.

SMART WORDS

adapt to change over time in order to survive in a certain environment

camouflage colors or patterns that help an animal blend in with its background

The well-camouflaged arctic hare is white in winter (below) and gray in summer (above). Its ears, which are short for members of the hare family, help it save body heat.

Keeping Warm

Animals of the tundra also have special ways to keep warm. One adaptation is thick hair or fur. The bighorn sheep of the alpine tundra grows two layers of hair. An inner layer traps air near its body. The air provides **insulation** to keep the sheep warm. An outer layer protects the sheep from wind and snow.

The musk ox, an arctic animal, also has a two-layered coat. It sheds the inner layer when the brief summer arrives.

The bighorn sheep is a majestic animal of the Rocky Mountains alpine tundra. The male's horns, which it uses for fighting, weigh up to 30 pounds (14 kilograms).

Polar bears are well adapted to the arctic tundra. Over a thick layer of blubber, they have black skin that soaks in the warmth of the sun. Their white fur keeps them camouflaged. But guess what? Their fur isn't really white! It's made up of clear, hollow hairs (left) that reflect light, making it look white.

Many arctic tundra animals have another way to keep warm. Polar bears, seals, and walruses have a thick layer of blubber. This stored fat can be several inches thick. It is another form of insulation. Blubber is especially important for animals that spend most of their time in cold arctic waters.

Blubber helps animals in another way, too. When food is hard to find, their bodies can break down blubber. It gives them the energy they need to survive.

SMART WORD

insulation something that slows the loss of heat

Hitting the Road

Tundra winters are too harsh for many animals, so they **migrate** to milder places. Caribou live in both arctic and alpine tundra lands, but they travel hundreds of miles to spend the winter in warmer forests.

Many birds travel south, too. The arctic tern migrates more than 10,000 miles (16,000 kilometers) to avoid the cold winters. The king eider duck spends its summers in the Arctic but travels to southern Alaska, eastern Canada, or New England for the winter.

The arctic tern has one of the animal world's longest migrations. It flies almost from one pole to the other!

SMART WORDS

migrate to travel from one region to another

hibernate to enter a deep sleep to save energy during harsh conditions

Some types of marmots hibernate for more than eight months. Imagine going more than half a year without eating a meal!

Staying In

Some animals stay in the tundra and **hibernate** through the winter. The arctic ground squirrel makes a nest in an underground burrow. In late summer, it fattens up on food and stores extra food in its nest. Then it goes into a deep sleep for many months. All of its body processes slow down. For instance, its body temperature becomes very low. This helps the squirrel save energy.

The marmot is an animal of the alpine tundra. Marmots do not store any food for hibernation. Instead, they stuff themselves with food before winter comes. The huge amount of fat they build up is used for energy while they sleep.

Strength in Numbers

Some tundra animals live in big groups. Staying together helps them block the strong winds and keep warm. It also helps keep predators away.

Tundra swans feed and travel in groups called **flocks**. They fly to the Arctic in May and early June. Tundra swans leave their flocks only to build nests. Then they lay eggs that hatch in about a month. A couple of months later, the swans gather again to migrate south before winter.

Tundra swans live in flocks. They sleep while they are floating, even in the winter.

Walruses of the Arctic live in large groups called **herds**. Walruses spend most of their time in the water, but sometimes they climb onto ice or rocky islands. During some parts of the year, they climb onto the land in one huge herd. Other times, males form a separate herd away from females and their young.

Elk are herding animals of the North American alpine tundra. Over time, human activities have pushed elk higher and higher into the mountains. But the survival of the elk shows us that life can find its way even in a shivery biome like the tundra.

SMART WORDS

flock a large group of birds

herd a large group of animals that live together

Answer each question with a Smart Word.

adapt	camouflage	insulation
migrate	hibernate	flock	herd

1. Which term describes something that slows the loss of heat?
2. Which term describes what animals do when they go through a deep, long period of sleep?
3. Which term describes what animals do when they travel to other places?
4. Which term describes what living things do when they change so they can survive?
5. Which term describes colors or patterns that help animals blend in with their surroundings?
6. Which term describes a group of land animals?
7. Which term describes a large group of birds?

Answers on page 32

Talk Like a Scientist

**Somebody shows you this picture of seals.
Use your Smart Words to describe how the
seals have adapted to life in the tundra.**

Did You Know?

Caribou, also called reindeer, are large members of the deer family. They live in huge herds of up to 100,000 animals. Caribou travel north to feed in the summer. Then they travel south in the winter.

That's Really Far!

Caribou can migrate up to 50 miles (80 kilometers) per day. Their large hooves spread apart to help them walk across snow and mud.

That's Amazing!

Newborn caribou can walk within an hour of being born. In just a few days, they can run with the herd.

Glossary

adapt to change over time in order to survive in a certain environment

alpine relating to high mountains

arctic relating to regions near the North Pole

biome a community of plants and animals that share a certain environment

camouflage colors or patterns that help an animal blend in with its background

climate the overall weather in a place over a long period of time

cushion plant a low-growing plant that forms clumps or mats

flock a large group of birds

glacier a huge, slow-moving mass of ice

global warming a trend of rising temperatures all over Earth

greenhouse effect what happens when gases surrounding Earth trap heat near the planet's surface

herd a large group of animals that live together

hibernate to enter a deep sleep to save energy during harsh conditions

ice sheet glacial ice that covers a large area of land

insulation something that slows the loss of heat

migrate to travel from one region to another

permafrost a layer of soil that is always frozen

tree line a boundary on a mountain above which trees do not grow

tundra a cold region with almost no trees and under 10 inches (25 centimeters) of precipitation each year

whiteout a condition when high winds pick up snow and blow it around quickly so everything looks white

Index

SMART WORDS Answer Key

p.10
1. climate, 2. biome, 3. tundra, 4. cushion plant, 5. alpine, 6. arctic, 7. glacier

p.18
1. global warming, 2. tree line, 3. permafrost, 4. greenhouse effect, 5. ice sheet, 6. whiteout

p.28
1. insulation, 2. hibernate, 3. migrate, 4. adapt, 5. camouflage, 6. herd, 7. flock